HISTORY FROM OBJECTS
TOYS

Karen Bryant-Mole

Wayland

HISTORY FROM OBJECTS

In The Home

Keeping Clean

At School

Toys

Clothes

In The Street

This edition published in 1996 by
Wayland (Publishers) Ltd

First published in 1994 by Wayland (Publishers) Ltd
61 Western Road, Hove, East Sussex, BN3 1JD, England

© Copyright 1994 Wayland (Publishers) Ltd

Edited by Deborah Elliott
Designed by Malcolm Walker

British Library Cataloguing in Publication Data
Bryant-Mole, Karen
   Toys. - (History From Objects Series)
   I. Title II. Series
   688.709

HARDBACK ISBN 0-7502-1020-6

PAPERBACK ISBN 0-7502-1898-3

Typeset by Kudos Editorial and Design Services
Printed and bound in Italy by G. Canale & C. S.p.A.

Notes for parents and teachers

This book has been designed to be used on many different levels.

It can be used as a means of comparing and contrasting objects from the past with those of the present. Differences between the objects can be identified. Such differences might include the shape, colour or size of the objects.

It can be used to look at the way designs have developed as our knowledge and technology have improved. Children can consider the similarities between the objects and look at the way particular design features have been refined. They can look at the materials that the objects are made from and the way they work. Modern goods are often made from modern materials such as plastic. Older mechanical objects are now frequently powered by electricity.

The book can be used to help place objects in chronological order and to help children understand that development in design corresponds with a progression through time.

It can also be used to make deductions about the way people in the past lived their lives. Children can think about how and why the objects might have been used and who might have used them. It is designed to show children that historical objects can reveal much about the past. At the same time it links the past with the present by showing that many of the familiar objects we use today have their roots planted firmly in history.

Contents

Some of the more difficult words which appear in **bold** are explained in the glossary on page 30.

Dolls

Dolls were one of the very first toys.

1900s

The doll's head and chest are made from papier-mâché. This is a hard **material** made from paper and glue. The doll's body and legs are made from fabric filled with straw.

1930s

This doll is made from felt. He has **joints** at his neck, the top of his arms and the top of his legs. This means that the parts of his body could be moved into different positions.

1950s

This doll looks more like a real person. Her eyes open and close. When her legs were moved, her head turned from side to side.

Can you see her little teeth?

Now

Today, many dolls are made from a very soft type of plastic. This doll has hair which can be washed and combed. She has a tiny tape recorder in a band on her wrist. This means she can repeat anything you record.

Teddy bears were named after Theodore Roosevelt, who was an American **president**. His nickname was Teddy.

1900s

This is a very old teddy bear. He has brown, button eyes. He looks as though he has been given new pads on his paws and feet. Can you see how long his arms are?

1930s

This looks more like a modern teddy bear. His arms are much shorter than the teddy from the 1900s. This teddy is filled with straw. He looks as though he's been cuddled a lot. His paws look worn and his fur is a bit thin.

1950s
This type of teddy is called a 'cheeky bear'. Do you think he looks cheeky? He has tiny bells in his ears which jingled when he was moved.

Now
Today, teddy bears have soft, man-made fillings. Some can even be washed. Teddy bears now come in lots of different designs and colours.

Doll's houses

A doll's house can be used to play lots of make-believe games.

1900s

This doll's house was not made by machines in a factory, it was made by hand. It looks like the real houses that were being built at that time. The inside of the house is very simple. There are no stairs or doorways between the rooms.

1930s

This type of doll's house was very popular. Most of the parts were made by machines. This meant that lots and lots of the same houses could be made at one time. There is a stairway inside the house, and doorways between the rooms. There are even lights with wires joined to a **battery**.
The battery made the lights work.

Now

Every part of this house is made in a factory. The house and everything in it is made from plastic. The two sides of the house close together and it can be carried around. Inside are lots of tiny copies of objects that we use at home. Can you spot a hair dryer, a cassette player and a telephone?

Family games

Games that can be played by the whole family have always been popular.

1910s

Here is a game of picture lotto.
Can you spot a bear, a pair of scissors
and a hot air balloon?

1950s

In this game small skittles were placed
in the gaps around the walls. The little
table in the middle of the game was
spun and this made the white ball shoot
about, bouncing off the walls and
knocking off the skittles.

1970s

The idea of this game was to win the other players' cones.
The game has a special dice shaker.
A player pressed down on the plastic dome in the middle of the game and the dice sprang around inside the dome.

Now

When the monkeys' tails are pressed the banana tree shakes and the monkeys' mouths open. The monkeys have to eat the bananas which fall off the tree. The game and the monkeys are made from brightly coloured plastic.

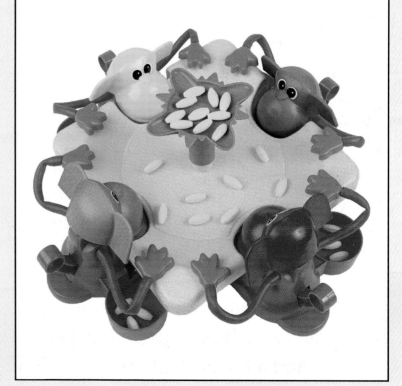

Train sets

Grown-ups and children love playing with train sets.

1910s

This is a home-made engine. It has been made from odds and ends which someone found around the house. Can you see some old boot polish tins and a candlestick?

1930s

This train set was made by a well-known company called Hornby. You can still buy Hornby train sets today. The train and its track are made from metal.

Now

Both the train and the track are made mostly from plastic. The coaches and the engine are joined by **magnets**. The pieces of the track are easy to fit together.

Tea sets

Children like to have tea parties for their dolls and teddy bears, so they need tea sets.

1890s

Here is a tea set made from very thin china, called bone china. It looks like a bone china tea set used by grown-ups. Bone china breaks very easily. Can you see that at some time one of the saucers has been mended?

1930s

This tea set is made from tin painted with enamel. Enamel is a special sort of paint which does not crack when it gets hot or wet. This tea set is light and unbreakable.

1960s

Here is another china tea set. This china is much thicker than the bone china and less likely to break. The bone china tea set had a pattern that looked like a grown-up's tea set. The pattern on this tea set was designed specially for children.

Now

Today, most children's tea sets are made from plastic. They come in all sorts of bright colours. This one even has its own tray.

TOYS Building sets

You can use building sets to make exciting and interesting models.

1910s

These stone building blocks are called Anchor Blocks. They come in different shapes, colours and sizes. The picture on the lid shows that the whole family could play with the bricks.

1940s

Bayko blocks are made from a material called bakelite, which is a type of hard plastic.
The blocks fitted on to metal pins. There are little doors, windows and even a roof.
A booklet came with the set. This showed children how to make lots of different buildings.

Now

Most children have used Lego at home or at school. You can buy lots and lots of different sets to make all kinds of models.

Toy prams

Teddy bears and dolls are pushed around in toy prams.

1890s
This pram looks just like the prams that babies were wheeled around in at that time. This is much smaller of course.
It would have been called a perambulator. The word perambulator has been shortened to pram.

1950s

This pram has a metal **frame**.
The pram is covered in plastic, which is waterproof. So with the hood up the doll would have kept dry even in the rain.

Now

Here is a pram covered in a soft material. The top can be lifted out and carried by blue handles.
The frame can then be folded flat.
The pram has a plastic shopping tray.

Toys on wheels

Some toys with wheels are pushed, while others are pulled.

1850s

Children could push themselves along on this wooden horse while holding on to the handle. Or, the handle could be pushed forward and someone else could pull them along.

1940s

Here is a push-along dog. Soft, push-along toy animals used to be very popular. This dog looks well-used, as it is a bit bald. The handle is quite low, so this toy was probably made for a very young child.

Now

This toy can be used in different ways. It is a push-along toy, and also a sit-and-ride toy.
The steering wheel turns the front wheels and there is a hooter.
The seat lifts up so that things can be stored underneath.

Hand-held games

These games can be carried around and played with anywhere.

1850s

Here is a wooden game called 'cup and ball'. A player held the handle part of the game and tried to flick the ball upwards, and make it balance on the small cup shape on the top of the handle.

1910s

This clown could do gymnastics. When the sticks were squeezed together the clown flipped around the rope at the top.

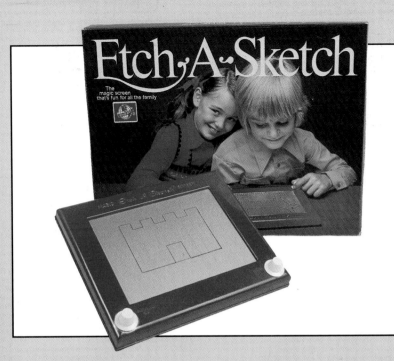

1970s

This is a picture drawing game. The knob on the left drew lines from one side of the screen to the other. The knob on the right drew the up and down lines. What has been drawn on the screen? You can still buy this game today.

Now

Here is a modern hand-held games computer. You can buy different games for it. The games are on discs which slot into the back. You use the buttons on the computer to move the figures and objects that come up on the screen.

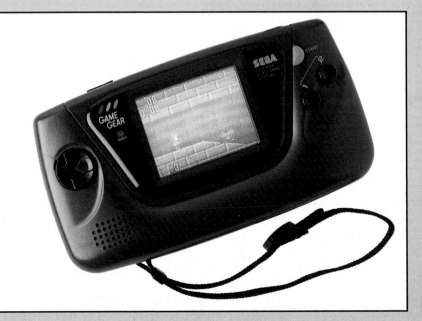

Clockwork toys

Children have always loved toys that 'do' things.

1920s

There is some clockwork machinery inside this cat. When the toy was wound up the cat started to move its arm as if it was playing the fiddle.

1930s

This is a character called Charlie Chaplin. It is made from tin covered with felt. The real Charlie Chaplin was an actor with a fast walk. When he walked he twirled his stick. When this toy was wound up it walked quickly and the stick twirled around.

1940s

Here is a toy hen made from tin. When the clockwork machinery inside it was wound up, the hen started to move. It looked as though it was pecking. When the clockwork wound down, it stopped.

Now

This game works by clockwork. The middle part of the game has to be twisted. This winds up the game. As it unwinds the middle part turns. The players have to try to flick the little balls into the spaces.

Toy cars

Cars are one of the most popular toys. Some children collect lots and lots of toy cars.

1910s

This clockwork car is made from tin. When it was wound up it moved by itself. Can you see how the black square towards the back has been painted to make it look like fabric?

1930s

Every part of this car is made from wood. The car does not have a roof. Cars like this are usually called sports cars.

1960s

This car has many more parts than the wooden car. The doors open, as do the **bonnet** and the boot. The car has windscreen wipers, lights and even a number plate.

Do you know what sort of car this is? It is a Rolls Royce.

Now

This is a radio-controlled car. Radio waves pass from a control box to the **aerial** on the car. You can use these radio waves to make the car move about.

Trikes

Trikes are vehicles with three wheels.

1920s

Almost all of this trike is made from metal. Only the seat and tyres are made from rubber. The seat could be moved forwards and backwards as well as up and down. The handlebars are an unusual curved shape. Can you see that there are no grips on the handlebars?

1950s

This trike has tyres which are filled with air. There is a carrier on the back of the trike where toys or books could be stored.
There are white plastic grips on the handlebars.

Now

This brightly coloured trike has plastic wheels, pedals and hand grips.
A friend could stand on the platform at the back of the trike and have a ride.
Can you spot a bell on this trike?

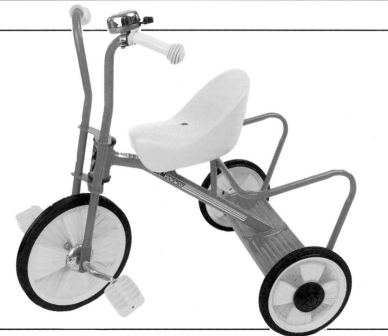

Glossary

aerial   a piece of wire that is used to pick up radio waves

battery   a machine which stores electricity and which is used to make things work

bonnet   the metal cover over the engine of a car

frame   metal pieces fitted together to give shape to something

joints   where two parts are joined together

magnets   pieces of iron or steel which draw other bits of iron or steel to them

material   what something is made from

president   the person who is in charge of a country

1850 S	1860 S	1870 S	1880 S	1890 S	1900 S	1910 S	1920 S

Books to read

History From Photographs series by Kath Cox and Pat Hughes (Wayland, 1995-6)
How We Used To Live, 1902-1926 by Freda Kelsall (A & C Black, 1985)
How We Used To Live, 1954-1970 by Freda Kelsall (A & C Black, 1987)
People Through History series by Karen Bryant-Mole (Wayland, 1996)
Starting History series by Stewart Ross (Wayland, 1991)

The illustration below is a timeline. The black and white drawings are of all the objects you have seen photographed in this book. Use the timeline to work out which objects came earlier or later than others, and which were around at the same time.

1930 S	1940 S	1950 S	1960 S	1970 S	1980 S	NOW

Index

Acknowledgements
The Publishers would like to thank the following people and organizations, which supplied the objects used in this book:
Gamleys Ltd 5 (right), 7, 9 (bottom), 13 (bottom), 15 (bottom), 17 (bottom), 21 (right), 27 (bottom); Mr & Mrs W.W. Bryant 4 (both), 5 (left), 8, 9 (top), 10 (right), 11 (left), 14 (both), 15 (top), 18, 21 (left), 24 (right), 25 (top); Norfolk Museums Services 10 (left), 12, 13 (top), 16, 17 (top), 19 (left), 20, 22 (both), 24 (left), 26 (both), 27 (top); Sussex Toy and Model Museum, Brighton 6 (both); L.E. Rigden Cycles, Brighton 28. All photographs are by Zul Mukhida except: 10 (left), 12, 13 (top), 16, 17 (top), 19 (left), 20, 22 (both), 24 (left), 26 (both), 27 (top), which are by GGS Photographic.